HEALING REFLECTIONS

for Parents of Estranged Adult Children

Guided Meditations
& Journaling Prompts
to Find Your Way Forward

SHERI McGREGOR, M.A.

ISBN: 978-0-9973522-9-0 (print)

Sowing Creek Press
Shingle Springs, CA 95692
info@sowingcreekpress.com
www.SowingCreekPress.com

DISCLAIMER:
This book is not a substitute for medical, spiritual, legal, or psychological advice. Content is based on the author's personal experience, as well as studies and research, but is the author's opinion. Readers should contact a licensed physician, psychiatrist, psychologist, or other licensed practitioner for diagnosis and care, or an attorney for legal advice. Although care was taken to ensure the research and information in this book was correct at the time it went to press, the author and publisher do not assume and hereby disclaim any liability to any party for loss, damage, or disruption due to any errors or omissions—whether the result of negligence, accident, or any other cause.

Cover and page design/layout by Lorie DeWorken, MindtheMargins.com

PRAISE FOR *HEALING REFLECTIONS*

A lovely opportunity to reflect deeply on a painful journey at a level only images can reach, and to come through with courage, insight and healing.

—DR. DINA GLOUBERMAN, groundbreaking pioneer of transformational imagery, author of *Life Choices, Life Changes*; *The Joy of Burnout*; and *ImageWork: The Complete Guide to Working with Transformational Imagery.*

Sheri McGregor wields her impressive powers of observation and description with great success in *Healing Reflections for Parents of Estranged Adult Children,* her self-help book of guided meditations and journaling prompts. She skillfully draws the reader into the imagined scene, allowing calm reflection that leads to contemplating small but steady changes in attitude. Trying to force wet wood to burn creates smoke but no flame. When might stepping back, rather than pushing harder, be a wiser course of action? Imagine a houseplant leaning toward a sliver of light at the edge of a curtained window. What new growth has begun to emerge in you, no matter how small? The 22 reflections in this book allow readers, privately and comfortably, to discover unlimited insights into how to view situations with new awareness.

—DIANE DIEKMAN, author of several biographies, including *Randy Travis: Storms of Life* and *Twentieth Century Drifter: The Life of Marty Robbins*. Her books and newsletters can be found at http://dianediekman.com.

Sheri McGregor gently guides parents of estranged adult children on a multi-sensory, illuminating and healing journey of the soul with her latest, empowering workbook. Filled with detailed imagery and introspective action steps, *Healing Reflections for Parents of Estranged Adult Children: Guided Meditations and Journaling Prompts to Find Your Way Forward* pairs masterful poetic writing with thoughtful observations of the natural world, blending the author's previously acclaimed collections on the wonder of nature with her multi-award winning *"Done With The Crying"* series of books. This is a must-have resource to help parents find peace as they move forward towards healing, growth and self-actualization while navigating the emotional pain associated with adult child estrangement.

—DR. MARNI HILL FODERARO, author of *Parental Alienation* and the award-winning *True Deceit False Love* series.

CONTENTS

INTRODUCTION 1

ONE   Your Sacred Fountain 5

TWO   Your Hidden Forest 15

THREE   Your Heart's Response 25

FOUR   Light in a Low Place 35

FIVE   Within the Waves 45

SIX   Solid Ground 55

SEVEN   What's Left Behind 65

EIGHT   Where Pressure Finds a Path 75

NINE   Your Inner Well 85

TEN   Where Drops Take Shape 95

ELEVEN   When Warm Meets Cold 105

TWELVE   The Light You Carry 115

THIRTEEN   After the Fire 125

FOURTEEN   Your Hearth Glows 135

FIFTEEN   What Won't Catch 147

SIXTEEN   The Wind That Lifts You 159

SEVENTEEN   When Light Appears 169

EIGHTEEN   Your Cloudscape 179

NINETEEN   What Grows? 189

TWENTY   Another Way 199

TWENTY-ONE   What's Near Is Enough 211

TWENTY-TWO   Higher Ground 221

Where You Stand: Integrating What You've Noticed . . . 231

About the Author 239

Explore More of Sheri McGregor's Work 241

INTRODUCTION

BEFORE YOU BEGIN: A NOTE ON APPROACH

In the early "daze" of estrangement, you may feel as if you're walking through a fog. Trouble concentrating, sudden tears, or feeling numb are common. Familiar joys collect burdens because holidays and special anniversaries take on weight and require new navigation skills. Even though estrangement is becoming more publicly discussed, you may still feel cautious when meeting new people, wondering what questions will be asked and how you'll answer. Relationships can feel stickier and less assured.

As time goes on, you grow more accustomed to stepping forward and living with hope while moderating expectations. One good moment of connection doesn't promise the next. False starts, guilt over what a parent "should" do, and messages echoed by relatives, society, or so-called experts can lead to bewilderment or resignation.

The nature of estrangement is ambivalent. A twist here, a new realization there—and sometimes a sudden cliff of despair. An uphill climb may give way to going with the flow. Or a river of tears leads to determination and strength. *Healing Reflections* will meet you wherever you are on a given day.

Through gentle imagery, brief reflection prompts, and simple sensory practices, you'll be helped to reconnect with yourself. Many clients and participants in my *Done With The Crying* membership describe this imaginal work as stepping into a quiet, restorative space—a pause that supports healing. You won't be asked to analyze your estrangement, justify decisions, or explain what happened. Those stories precede the healing and inner strength that can grow from living beyond them.

Each reflection invites you to enter a symbolic space: a courtyard, a clearing, a patch of sunlight...

WHY IMAGERY?

When you vividly imagine yourself inside a scene, your brain responds as if you're experiencing the moment. The same physical and emotional calming that comes with spotting a rainbow in the mist, inhaling the rich, earthy smell of a forest, or hearing the flutter of a bird's wings can occur. The use of imagery can regulate emotion, reduce distress, and support positive change.[1,2]

The symbolic, emotionally evocative, and sensory-rich imagery in the pages ahead provides a soft entry point to insight rather than attacking the pain of loss head-on. Calm reflection can elicit flashes of understanding that help you view the pain of your broken relationship(s) from a new angle, promoting flexibility and growth. This approach helps sidestep negative rumination, so you gain insight and momentum with ease.[1,2]

Some people find it helpful to experience the written scenes as spoken

---

1 Pearson J., Naselaris T., Holmes E. A., & Kosslyn S. M. (2015). *Mental imagery: Functional mechanisms and clinical applications.* Nature Reviews Neuroscience, 16(9), 611–626.
2 Skottnik L., & Linden D. E. J. (2019). *Mental imagery and brain regulation—New links between imagery, cognition and emotion.* Frontiers in Psychiatry, 10, 779.

meditations, especially those they want to revisit. For that reason, audio recordings are available at my website (**www.RejectedParents.Net/audios**). To benefit fully from the spoken meditation, immerse yourself while resting or sitting quietly, then return to the prompts in the book.

ENTERING THE REFLECTIVE PROCESS

Each entry in *Healing Reflections* starts with a brief factual opening and a calming reminder to relax and engage before a meditative scene invites you into your inner world and wisdom. These images are not meant to be decoded or solved but experienced as metaphors that allow insight to arise indirectly. Ideally, you would move sequentially through the book at a leisurely pace—reading one scene, imagining yourself inside it, and then pondering the reflection prompts and writing your responses. Take your time with each meditation, perhaps revisiting it over several days, and reflect upon individual questions or a few at a time. Journaling can be a slow process. Insight may be revealed in layers as you cycle back and till new emotional terrain over time. Honor the process.

You might find yourself drawn to a single detail in a guided scene: a bench, a trailing vine, or the sound of wind rustling through trees. This imagery meets you where you are. Choosing what draws you in is an important part of the process. Estrangement can leave even the most capable people feeling powerless, caught in a storm they didn't choose. Here, your choices matter. You notice what calls to you, which questions to answer, and how deeply you go. The freedom to direct yourself is part of reclaiming your strength, identity, and power.

To help you embody calm awareness and integrate your experiences as you move through your reflections, a short, sensory micro-practice follows each reflection prompt. These easy practices help you more fully embody the ideas and benefit from the metaphors or elements of nature presented. Though brief, these contemplative practices can reduce stress and support emotional balance as they help you reconnect with peace and possibility.[3]

Feel free to doodle in the space provided as well. Simple marks and repeating lines, complete sketches, or shapes and icons you draw intuitively can curb mental drifting and improve recall. Doodling engages the mind differently than words alone because the gentle movement of the hand provides an attentional anchor. This can help people stay present while reflecting. No need to create masterpieces. This is for you and about honoring the impromptu art of your life.[3]

A NOTE FOR YOUR JOURNEY

As you spend time in *Healing Reflections*, don't worry about a specific outcome. You're not being rushed into a reconciliation formula or onto a path to a mythical oasis of closure. This is *your* journey, and time well spent. How you experience the meditative imagery, combined with your unique insights distilled via the reflection prompts and practices, is meant to help you find and reclaim yourself more fully.

Welcome to *your* healing reflections—*as they unfold for you*.

---

3 Andrade J. (2009). *What does doodling do?* Applied Cognitive Psychology, 23(8), 1040–1045.

one

YOUR SACRED FOUNTAIN

Fountains have long symbolized the flowing nature of people's lives—the emotional elements collecting, bubbling forth, and circling back again. Across cultures, fountains mark the pulse of a lively town square or form the heart of a quiet, contemplative space where troubles are carried in and left behind. The cycling water echoes the nature of renewal and release. When your heart feels dry, even a trickle of movement can begin to restore hope.

Now, settle into your seat. Draw in a slow breath and let it out with an audible sigh. Inhale again, exhale softly, and let your body ease. Relax your shoulders. Feel your feet on the floor. Allow yourself to arrive fully at this moment.

Now, imagine ... a courtyard tucked behind an old stone archway and, in its center, a fountain. Perhaps it's formal, with tiered bowls and a deep basin. Or maybe your fountain is a series of pouring vessels, or a single bubbling stone. Imagine the sound. Does it reverberate? Is it soft? Rushing? Or just a trickle?

You sit on a shaded bench and listen—both lulled and enlivened in this sacred space. A vine has climbed over the wall, stretching tendrils toward the water. A bit of moss grows at the fountain's base. The air is moist and refreshing, the ambient water sounds echoing against the courtyard walls. Dappled light filters through the trees, gentling you into a meditative stupor.

A bird begins to sing from a nearby limb. Its repeating call stirs something in you—perhaps familiar or entirely new.

What arises? A feeling, an image, a memory? Jot down your thoughts and impressions.

⟡ NOTICE WHAT STANDS OUT

As you imagine this courtyard fountain, what draws your attention?

- the sound of water—rushing, playful, trickling
- the bench, shaded and waiting
- the vine or moss, clinging to what sustains it
- the bird, expressing itself
- or something else

Linger with the imagery for a moment. What thoughts or memories emerge? Draw or write about whatever comes up for you.

⁓ REFLECT

1. Emotional flow shifts under strain. *When you feel vulnerable, discon-nected, or uncertain, how does your own "flow" shift? Where do you notice slowing, stopping, or strain? What might help you begin moving again, even a little?*

2. Whatever detail in the scene draws your attention holds meaning. *What might that detail mirror—or perhaps contrast—about where you're at emotionally right now?*

3. Patterns form around our protection and survival. *When you've faced hurt, loss, or other emotional wounding in the past, how have you tended to respond—by reaching, resting, clinging, or calling out? How might that pattern help or limit you now?*

4. Fountains move in elegant cycles: gathering, rising, releasing. *Where do you sense renewal or letting go in this season of your life? Is some emotional movement happening beneath the surface?*

5. Release creates space. *If you could visit this sacred fountain space, what would you bring in ... and leave behind? How might setting down those burdens open space for something new to flow in?*

TUNING IN

Find or imagine the sound of water: a running faucet, raindrops pelting dry earth, or even an audio recording. Breathe easily as you listen for a minute or two. Let the rhythm remind you that movement doesn't have to mean rushing forward. Sometimes healing begins by returning to yourself, and even a trickle can signal renewal.

two

YOUR HIDDEN FOREST

In woodlands throughout the world, mushrooms spring up suddenly when cool air, moisture, or a subtle seasonal shift make conditions right. These delicate, strange, or surprisingly bold fungi are only the visible part of a much bigger system. Beneath every cap or cluster is a vast mycelial network that's hidden from view. Intricate threads break down fallen leaves, branches, and other matter. What has reached its living end is transformed into nourishment for what grows next.

This unseen work mirrors the expression of our inner lives. Tender emotional "fruitings" like longing or regret may rise when conditions are ripe. Stress, exhaustion, or an anniversary may stir a familiar ache that prompts outburst or withdrawal. Like the mycelium, your internal ecosystem notices and responds, even when you're not fully aware of why.

Settle into your body. Draw in a slow, calming breath ... and let it go with a sigh. Take another breath, letting your shoulders droop. Feel the weight of your legs and notice your feet touching the ground. Let your breath find a natural rhythm, steady and unhurried.

Now, breathing softly, imagine... walking along a shaded woodland path just after a cool rain. The air carries the earthy scent of wet leaves and fertile soil. You move slowly, delighting in deepened greens, rich browns, and wet stones that are newly vibrant. Wind swirls and gusts before settling into an audible hush. A squirrel scratches for lost acorns in fallen leaves. Birds chirp, happy in their after-storm flights.

Ahead, pale light filters through the treetops, and you notice a small gathering of mushrooms rising from the softened ground. A bigger, thicker mushroom stands tall beside a fallen log. Nearby, a delicate cluster fans out near the base of a tree. A round, table-flat cap catches your eye, whimsical enough to stir childlike wonder.

You bend for a closer look and marvel at their textures—smooth, pocked in places, corrugated underneath. Some rise strong from clumps of disturbed earth they've pushed aside. Others are delicate, stretching weblike from a dusting of fallen leaves. You imagine the vast networks beneath your feet, quietly transforming what has ended into what will become something new.

A drop of rain falls from a high branch and wets your cheek. You pause in the stillness, aware of the living forest before you ... and the hidden forest within you.

What thoughts, memories, or sensations come to mind? Does the scene evoke tenderness, curiosity, unease, or something familiar from your own emotional seasons? Spend a few minutes with your impressions, however simple or layered they may be.

NOTICE WHAT STANDS OUT

As you imagine walking this wet woodland path, what draws your attention?

- the softened earth and deepened colors after rain
- the lone mushroom rising next to the fallen log
- the delicate cluster near the tree's base, growing in community
- the flat, whimsical cap that stirred a sense of childhood wonder
- the awareness of unseen threads beneath your feet
- or something else . . .

Linger with what is vivid to you.

⌥ CONSIDER

1. Many describe estrangement as being "always present" even when it's not their focus. *What emotions or memories "surface" for you un-expectedly at certain times? What inner or outer conditions seem to bring them out?*

2. Fungi comes in a wide variety of forms and shapes. *Thinking of the mushrooms in the scene, what does their form—solitary, clustered, delicate, strong, whimsical—mirror about you right now?*

3. A vast network of mycelium transforms fallen matter into new soil. *What might be unfolding for you? What beliefs, roles, or expectations might be softening, breaking down, or preparing to change?*

4. Some mushrooms push up with force, disturbing earth. Others more gently flex and stretch, almost unnoticed. *When do you push through, withdraw, soften, or seek connection? How has that served you—or not?*

5. In nature, what has reached maturity is released—yet utilized for enrichment. *Given your circumstances, what might you leave on the forest floor? What burden, story, role, or expectation could return to the earth? What might grow in its place?*

REMEMBERING CAPACITY

If possible, step outside for a moment or to a window. Close your eyes and bathe in the natural light. Imagine the scent of damp earth, reminding you that life is always shifting. For a few minutes, breathe softly as you picture a forest floor and, beneath, the hidden threads of life at work. With each breath, affirm that you are more than your rising emotions at any given time. You are the whole forest, roots, soil, and hidden systems with the capacity for renewal.

three

YOUR HEART'S RESPONSE

High in the sky, hail forms amid turbulence. As air surges and shifts, raindrops are lifted into a storm cloud, dropped, and then lifted again. With each up-and-down shift, a new layer of ice sticks, building into frozen hail. The more turbulent the storm, the more the cycle repeats. What began as raindrops grows larger and harder. When the turbulence quiets, the hail falls to the earth where it collects and eventually melts away.

Now, sit comfortably, draw in a breath, and release it. Let your tongue rest at the bottom of your mouth as you breathe easily. Relax and feel your body let down its guard. You're here in this moment. There is nowhere else you need to be.

Now, breathe easily and imagine ... you're sheltered on a covered porch, looking out at the steel-wool sky. The air is cold, and you stuff your hands into your jacket pockets. A sudden ping on the metal gutter startles you to attention. There's another ping—and then the sky lets loose. Before you, hail falls hard and heavy. The icy beads pile in the grass and form drifts around bushes. Just as suddenly as the clatter started, the hailstorm ends. All is still. You look out, noticing how different the landscape looks. The white drifts look solid, but you know how quickly they can melt. How long will the cold sustain them?

What thoughts come to mind? Memories, imaginings, or emotions—jot them down. Perhaps a phrase arises, or even a single word. Write whatever stirs in you now.

⌒⌐ NOTICE WHAT STANDS OUT

As you picture the hailstorm, notice what draws your attention.

- the upward lift, brief and hopeful
- the sudden drop, sharp and jarring
- the hard shell, formed layer by layer
- the storm itself, unpredictable, perhaps exhausting
- something else entirely

Pause with what caught your attention before moving on.

REFLECT

1. Hail forms through repeated lifting and dropping. *When did you feel lifted in hope and then dropped in disappointment?* (Feel free to describe this pattern in your own words.)

2. Each freeze-and-thaw cycle adds more ice. *What emotional layers have built up around you? Are they protective, numbing, or both?*

3. The storm shapes the hail, but at its heart, it's still water. *In what ways did the unpredictability of your adult child's behavior shape your responses? How are you the same?*

4. Hail eventually melts. *When you imagine allowing your emotional guarding to thaw, what might begin to shift in how you feel and how you see the world and live?*

5. Every hailstone bears a history of repetition. *Where in the repeated patterns of estrangement can you step aside, soften, or interpret in ways that help you?*

WORKING WITH CONDITIONS

Drop an ice cube into hot water or hold a small piece of ice in the warmth of your hand. Notice how effortlessly the ice begins to soften and melt. Rest in the truth that "hardening your heart" against further hurt doesn't make you "cold-hearted." You are not required to stay frozen, nor are you required to melt on command. You can weigh conditions and work with them.

four

LIGHT IN A LOW PLACE

Puddles form in low spots after rain. Some are absorbed by the ground or evaporate quickly in sunlight. Others linger, collecting mud and debris where the land dips and holds them. Though impermanent, even a puddle can host new life: reeds spring forth, mosquito larvae proliferate, and tadpoles hatch. Birds feast in their ephemeral abundance. No matter how small or fleeting, a puddle reflects the sky.

Take a slow, easy breath ... and let it go. Feel where your body meets the chair or whatever is supporting you. Continuing to breathe, relax your brows and your gaze. Yawn purposely and soften your jaw. Be here now—fully present in this moment.

Now, breathing softly, imagine ... you're walking a familiar nature path on the first sunny day after a series of rainstorms. The air is fresh with the smell of damp earth. In the distance ahead, a bird on the path startles, chirps once, and flies away. *What was it doing on the path?* As you step closer, you notice a large puddle. So that's what the bird was interested in.

You stop where water has gathered in a wide, shallow dip in the ground. Around the edges, shiny mud holds tiny bird tracks. At one edge, the mud is thick and some debris has gathered: a seed pod, a tangle of dry grass, a few pebbles. Then you notice something else and, squatting for a closer look, marvel at tiny green sprigs poking up from the water—life finding a way. You notice the puddle is full of light, its smooth, still surface reflecting puffy white clouds in a blue sky. As a breeze caresses your cheek, tiny ripples drift on the water. At the puddle's edge, something wriggles: a fat tadpole, coming up for air.

What thoughts or impressions arise? Jot down a phrase, image, or emotion.

⟞⟎ NOTICE WHAT STANDS OUT

As you imagine the puddle, what draws your attention?

- the lower ground that invites water to collect
- the mud and debris
- the life that's nurtured
- the reflection of the sky
- other details

Allow yourself to linger with and expand on this scene. Are you more drawn to what's reflected by or collected here? What else might be here for you? Doodle and write about what comes up for you.

⟿ CONSIDER

1. Puddles form in low areas where water is caught. *When, if ever, have you felt stuck with no clear path forward? What feelings lingered with you?*

2. Some puddles are absorbed or evaporate quickly. *Which of your emotions or loops of thought fade away easily? Which tend to stick and gather "debris"? What situations do these feelings* reflect?

3. Even in stagnant spots, new life appears. *What activities or attitudes have become "new life" for you? Think:* new interests, moments of peace, and shifts in viewpoint. *Can you savor their brief abundance?*

4. We may walk past a puddle without much notice, even as wildlife appreciates the nourishment it holds. *When/where have you found unexpected comfort, validation, or support—even if transient in nature? Where can you seek out more of this?*

5. Puddles reflect the sky. *When you look into your own "low places,"*
    what larger truth, strength, or persistence do you see reflected there
    about who you are—and how you've endured?

6. Puddles are often easy to step around, especially when the path continues on. *What feelings, memories, or insights have you learned to move past quickly—whether small or significant—that may be asking for your attention now?*

WHAT GATHERS

If possible, step outside and look for rises, dips, or hollows in the ground. If there's a puddle nearby, pause and reflect upon it for a moment. If not, imagine your puddle in a low spot, reflecting a gorgeous sky. Place your palm over your heart and breathe easily. Even low places can hold life and light.

five

WITHIN THE WAVES

The vast expanse of an ocean is humbling and comforting. It's the keeper of mysteries, yet as rhythmic as calming breath. Fed by rivers, rain, and melting ice, the sea gathers waters from every direction and carries them around the world. Saltwater both heals and stings—a paradox. Healing after estrangement can feel like that too: the steps that soothe us sometimes also hurt. The ocean's hidden depths hold treasures, migrations, and the promise of discovery. Yet, at times, its power can be frightening.

Settle into your seat. Soften your gaze as if looking out over the ocean. *Can you hear its breath?*

Now, imagine ... standing with the cool, damp sand beneath your feet and the horizon stretching endlessly before you. The waves roll in and out, steady and rhythmic. Each one curls toward you and thins into foam, then sweeps away to rejoin the greater body. *Is that a ship in the distance?* Held in the sea's velvety roar, you crane your neck and squint, confirming the dark outline of a distant mast in the sun's setting glow.

A gull's cry pierces the air, and you look up as it passes, the salty breeze ruffling your hair. The sea's spell broken, you step along, continuing your walk as waves foam at your feet, tugging at sun-warmed kelp. As the water washes out, the sands are sifted away, revealing shells like the ocean's offered secrets.

What thoughts or impressions arise? A word, an image, a memory? Jot it down.

◦ NOTICE WHAT STANDS OUT

As you imagine standing on the shoreline, notice what draws your attention.

- the steady rhythm of the waves
- the shimmering horizon stretching beyond sight
- the shells left behind
- the pull of the tide—coming close, and then withdrawing
- something else

Let your thoughts linger with what captures your attention.

∽ REFLECT

1. Waves move with steady rhythm, shaped by forces larger than themselves. They don't question their strength. They simply rise, curl, and return. *What internal rhythm carries you forward even when relationships feel uncertain or unreachable? Where do you feel most "yourself" and most grounded?*

2. The ocean collects water from many sources. *What streams are feeding you right now?* Think: supportive people, new interests, rest, insight, or even hard-won lessons. *Which currents feel turbulent or draining? What small adjustments could help rebalance the mix?*

3. Oceans can mesmerize us—the horizon, the roar, the endless motion. Yet a single gull's cry can break the spell and help us move forward. *Where have you felt caught up in worry, replaying the past, or searching for answers? What helps break that spell so you can step forward again?*

4. Over time, the pounding of the waves reshapes the shoreline. *What subtle shifts in your understanding, boundaries, or resilience do you notice have been shaped by repeated experiences in estrangement?*

5. Every wave leaves behind a shell, a pattern in the sand, a polished stone... *What bits of insight or unexpected gifts have you gathered as you've navigated the tides of loss and uncertainty? How might you honor and hold onto them?*

BREATHING WITH THE WAVES

Sit quietly and imagine waves rolling in and out. Sync your breath with the waves. Inhale as they rise, exhale as they release. Tell yourself softly: *You don't have to control the whole ocean. Just meet each moment as it comes. Let them wash over you.*

six

SOLID GROUND

Earthquakes begin deep underground where pressure builds between tectonic plates that are always moving. Friction causes stress that accumulates and eventually demands release. That's when the shaking happens. When the main quake settles, smaller aftershocks occur over days or months. These jarring reminders are unpredictable and often keep people on edge. Relational ruptures have similar lingering and unexpected tremors.

Soften your gaze and take a breath ... as you exhale, imagine any tension swirling out and away from you. Relax your brows, your tongue, your neck .... sit comfortably, noticing where your body meets what's supporting it.

Now, imagine you're in a quiet room ... sunlight filters in through the window curtain. The air is still. You are at peace and grateful. Suddenly, you hear a faint roar, and a subtle vibration ripples through the floor. The lamp trembles. A picture frame on the wall rattles. Just as your mind registers "earthquake," the trembling stops—but your nerves stand at attention, flexed and ready. You quickly glance around, letting out your pent-up breath. Your framed picture hangs off center. You're relieved the quake is over, but you're still on alert, ready to act.

As you sit with this scene, do you notice any parallels in your life? What thoughts, memories, or feelings come to mind?

◦ NOTICE WHAT STANDS OUT

As you picture this earthquake scene, what draws your attention?

- the faint roar
- the shock of what's happening
- your body's echoing tremor
- the subsequent stillness
- the unease of what may still be coming
- something else

Pause for a moment, tuning in to your responses.

⌒∘ CONSIDER

1. We encounter earthquakes without warning. Describe parallels in your relational experience. *What moments have felt sudden and disorienting? What came out of nowhere?*

2. Earthquakes occur along fault lines where there's pressure or where previous ruptures have occurred. *What, if any, "pressures" do you recognize or speculate may have preceded the rupture with your adult child? How does noticing or naming any pressure shift your perspective or validate what you've already sensed?*

3. Aftershocks are unpredictable and can cloud the future with apprehension. *In your experience, what "aftershocks" such as brief contact, mixed messages, or unexpected blame have occurred? How have these events influenced your outlook or daily life?*

4. An earthquake leaves the surroundings altered. Perhaps subtly, like a tilted picture on the wall. Or, in bigger ways, such as fallen buildings or broken glass. *What parts of your life feel shaken, cracked, or rearranged since the estrangement? How have these shifts been difficult? Which disruptions have revealed unexpected strength or clarity?*

5. Rebuilding includes reinforcing what still stands and clearing away what cannot be restored to allow for new growth. *What remains solid in you? How might you reinforce those strengths? What requires acceptance and release?*

6. Even with an expectation of aftershocks, communities and people adapt and get on with living. *Using the earthquake-aftershock metaphor as an example, how can you regain your footing? What helps you feel safe?*

STEADY GROUND

Stand with your feet flat on the floor, noticing its support. Inhale slowly and, on the exhale, assure yourself of your strength and ability to adapt. Use phrases that fit your journey and feel truest. Something like:

- *You're still standing.*
- *Your foundation is strong.*
- *You're finding your footing.*
- *You're stepping along on firmer ground now.*

Breathing easily and with longer outbreaths than inbreaths, repeat your phrase(s) several times.

seven

WHAT'S LEFT BEHIND

As the ocean's tides respond to the gravitational pull of the sun and moon, waves slide further inland. When the tide recedes, pools of seawater remain in pockets carved into the rocks of the intertidal zone. Fish and other marine life are temporarily trapped in these pools, surviving despite shifting temperatures, exposure to sunlight, and dwindling oxygen. Crabs skitter into tiny crevices to hide until the tide returns. Some creatures—like barnacles—don't *get* stuck so much as *stick*, fastening themselves in place despite the rise and fall of the tides.

Take a breath and rest in your chair. Let your shoulders drop and your jaw go slack. Breathe softly and focus your attention on this moment—right here where you sit.

Now, *imagine* ... a partly cloudy day on the seashore. A steady wind carries gliding pelicans and a scattering of gulls. The tide is out, and you walk toward a rocky area you know holds wonder: tidepools. As sand gives way to jagged rock, you step carefully. A fidgety crab scuttles sideways out of sight. You bend to peer into a small pool. Beneath the clear, trapped water you spot rusty red sea lettuce—a punch of color against the dark stone. Nearby, a plump sea cucumber rests in a shallow hollow. A colony of sea anemones crowds one rock face, their fleshy, silver-blue tendrils in full bloom.

You stand and notice more anemones, ranging from the size of a quarter to the span of your palm, anchored fast all along the pitted rock. Stepping carefully, you move to another shallow pool, this one lined with soft white sand. A shell moves, jerking awkwardly across the bottom. You blink and laugh, realizing it's a hermit crab carrying its borrowed home.

What comes to you in picturing these tidepools? A thought, a memory, an image, a feeling?

NOTICE WHAT STANDS OUT

As you imagine these tidepools, what draws your attention?

- the creatures waiting for the tide to return
- barnacles and anemones that hold fast through changing conditions
- the clarity of the water, revealing worlds of life
- glimmers of color against dark, pitted rock
- something else

Pause here with what stands out.

⟲ REFLECT

1. Tidepools form when the water pulls away, leaving life exposed and vulnerable. *When, in the season of estrangement, or another time in your life, have you felt left behind and uncertain what would happen next? What feelings surface when you think about those low-tide moments?*

2. Some tidepool creatures cling tightly, others hide, and some simply endure until conditions change. *Which of these survival responses feels familiar to you? How has it helped you navigate estrangement? How might it now be wearing you down?*

3. In tidepools, life continues even in constrained spaces. *What new life (interests, strength, insight, or connections) has begun to appear in your in-between times? How might you nurture one of these beginnings?*

4. When the waves pull back, they reveal wonders that are easy to miss. Healing can be like that too. Brief glimmers appear before the next emotional tide returns. *What small moments of healing, stability, or relief have appeared for you recently? How might you savor these breakthrough moments and enjoy them a little longer?*

5. When the tides change, the pools are new again. Some creatures are carried back to the ocean, while others remain for another cycle. *Consider your own cycles of emotional ebb and flow. What are you ready to release to the larger "sea" of your life? What do you want to carry forward with you?*

NOTICING SHIFTS

Consult tide charts and, if you can, visit the seashore when the tide is low and again when it's high. Notice how the shore looks different. *How has it changed*? Write a list of contrasting words to describe the shore at low versus high tide. Consider which of these words may describe you at different times.

If you're unable to visit a shore in person, use your imagination.

eight

WHERE PRESSURE FINDS A PATH

When groundwater beneath the surface is heated by a chamber of magma deep within the earth, pressure builds. Seeking escape, the superheated water rises through cracks and channels in the rock. When the pressure is high and the path out narrow, a geyser releases the boiling water with force, sometimes rhythmically, like Yellowstone's Old Faithful. When the pathway is more open, the heated water rises gently into hot springs, releasing warmth and steam into the air. These geothermal vents act as natural valves, allowing heat and tension to escape steadily rather than build beneath the surface.

We might think of our emotional landscapes as having similar pockets of pressure. If we let off "steam" in steady, safe expressions, our emotions protect us. Just as the areas around mineral rich hot springs support new life, our emotional expressions, rising for gentle release, support our growth.

Gently roll your neck, first in one direction, and then the next, to relieve tension. Exhale with a soft sigh. Draw in another breath and relax.

Now, imagine ... you're walking a red-rock path on a brisk, autumn day. Ahead, you notice wispy steam rising into the air. A faint tinge of sulfur hits your nose. A few steps further and you spot a natural mineral pool near a red rock outcropping. You move closer, noticing the white rim at its edge, a crusting of minerals reminiscent of rustic pool tile. You gaze into the water, marveling at its brilliant blue, brighter than the sky. A soft hiss draws your attention to a nearby rocky rise where a ribbon of steam lifts into the air and disappears. You take a breath, awed by the world of heat and pressure hidden beneath the rock, and the earth's wisdom in releasing it.

What thoughts or impressions arise? Jot down a word, a memory, or whatever comes to mind.

⌒○ NOTICE WHAT STANDS OUT

As you imagine arriving at this hot spring, what draws you in?

- the bright blue of the spring water
- the hiss of the nearby steam vent
- the faint sulfur smell
- the ring of mineral crust circling the pool
- something else

Pause, allowing the images to settle into memory.

∽ CONSIDER

1. Deep beneath the earth, pressure builds long before anything rises to the surface. *Thinking of your estrangement, where have you felt pressure building before taking visible action in any way? What feelings, thoughts, or behavioral patterns alert you that something in yourself needs attention?*

2. Geothermal vents release heat and pressure, preventing larger ruptures. *In your own life, what actions work like "vents," helping you let
   off steam or safely express yourself? Which of these outlets might you
   choose to lean on more often?*

3. Hot springs release heat without eruption. In a similar way, anger can serve as a natural warning system, letting you know when you've been hurt, dismissed, or wronged. *What protective wisdom might anger offer? How could you allow that wisdom to guide your actions? In what way might anger be asking you to honor yourself?*

4. Consider the concept of "bottling up" emotions. *Where might you be holding in or perhaps dismissing your own emotions as unimportant, unwanted, or wrong? What shift, even a small one, could help you to admit your feelings, express yourself, or release?*

5. Over time, as minerals are deposited at the edges, hot spring pools deepen. *What emotional capacity or inner strengths, such as self-compassion, patience, understanding, or self-protection, have been expanding in you? How might you acknowledge these layers of depth and wisdom? How might you nurture them to sustain you?*

NATURAL RELEASE

As you move through your day, notice any warmth rising around you. Steam from a cup, a hot shower, or your dishwasher. The soft heat of clothes pulled from the dryer, or a mug of hot soup warming your hands. Pause for a purposeful breath in ... and a slow exhale. Let the heat be a reminder: the release of pressure can be natural and safe.

nine

YOUR INNER WELL

Deep underground, water that's naturally filtered through sand and stone collects in sheltered spaces. A well can access this life-giving reserve. With lowered buckets or simple pumps, people draw the water upward. Even in long, dry spells, a little effort reveals this hidden resource.

Feel your feet steady on the ground. Take an easy breath in ... and let it go. Notice yourself relaxing. A quiet place is waiting inside you.

Now, breathing easily, imagine ... you're walking a dusty path under bright mid-day sun. The once fertile land lies parched. Yellowed grass, the buzz of cicadas, and air so still it seems lifeless. You put one foot in front of the other, moving forward, but growing weary. Your mouth is dry. You've been walking for a long while and only now realize how thirsty you've become.

Around a bend, a green meadow opens before you. A slight breeze stirs the prairie grass, and colorful flowers dot the landscape. Up ahead, something draws your eye: a sturdy stone well. In the shade of a small, bright tree rests a wooden bucket. *Can it really be true?* You smile, grateful to see what appears to have been set there for travelers.

You step forward and, as your fingers touch the worn wooden bucket, something inside you stirs. This feels familiar. You've drawn from this sort of place before. As you lean over the rim and peer into the darkness, a hint of cool, still air bathes your face. You fasten the bucket to the pulley's hook and begin turning the handle. The rope creaks as the bucket descends, and the sound echoes up reassuringly. You smile, realizing the well has always been here. You've returned to it on long, dry walks more than once.

What thoughts, feelings, or memories surface here? Jot down a few words or sentences.

⟿ NOTICE WHAT STANDS OUT

As you imagine the scene, what stands out?

- the worn wooden bucket
- the parched stretch of land
- the buzzing cicadas
- the blooming meadow
- the refreshing cool rising from within the depths
- the sense of familiarity
- something else

Linger for a moment with whatever images drew you in.

⟿ REFLECT

1. Even in dry spells, a well holds abundance that has gathered over time. *When life feels dry or discouraging, what inner resources have carried you? How have you noticed those strengths supporting you even when you felt spent?*

2. Like drawing refreshing water with a bucket, taking care of yourself requires effort. *Where in your healing have you recognized you must make efforts to feel relief? What helps you "lower the bucket" instead of giving up?*

3. Surface storms don't touch a well's deep reserves. *What truths, beliefs, or parts of yourself remain with you no matter what your adult child does? How might returning to those values support you now?*

4. Drawing from a well requires trust that water exists, even when you can't see it. *In what ways are you learning to trust yourself? Where in your life do you most easily access clarity or your inner wisdom?*

5. The well in the scene has served you before. *What past experiences have shown you your resilience, even if you weren't certain you had the courage or strength needed at the time? How might your grit or determination help you now?*

REPLENISH WHAT'S YOURS

Do at least one thing today that genuinely replenishes you. That might mean pausing to rest in the shade, taking a drink of cool water, or enjoying a moment of sunlight on your back. As you do, interpret the intention: *You're refilling.* Celebrate it: *Good job taking care of yourself.* Savor these moments. Small refills count.

ten

WHERE DROPS TAKE SHAPE

Inside the secret chambers of caves around the world, strange formations emerge over centuries from water moving through rock. Mineral-rich water drips from a cave ceiling and leaves tiny deposits that harden into icicle-like stalactites. Where drops land and minerals accumulate, stalagmites grow from the cave floor. Sometimes the built-up minerals meet, forming a single column. Cave interiors may also be draped in flowstone, sometimes called "draperies," and named for waterfalls such as the Frozen Niagara in Kentucky's Mammoth Cave. Like petrified waterfalls or rain, these formations create ethereal, sometimes fragile, shapes in the darkness, hidden from sight.

As you contemplate this idea, gently roll your neck and shoulders. Settle in and notice what's supporting your body: your back, your seat, your feet…. Let your breath find a natural rhythm as you fully relax.

Now, breathing steadily, imagine ... stepping into the cool entrance of a dimly lit cavern—one of those echoing caves you might find in a national park. As you move along the pathway behind others, your hand glides along the cool metal rail. Soft walkway lights glow at your feet. You hear the hushed *oohs* and *ahs* of those ahead of you. When the path curves and the cavern opens into a wide chamber, you pause, gazing at the scene. Your breath catches at the sight.

Soft lighting reveals delicate and strangely beautiful mineral formations. Graceful stalactites taper from the ceiling like dripped candle wax. Below them, stalagmites rise from the floor, meeting in places to form glistening columns, the artifacts of time. Along one wall, rippled flowstone hangs like a frozen waterfall, its surface glossy in the glowing light.

You lean against the rail, noticing the faintest echoing of drips—time still moving, drops hardening into the earth's bones. You stand there, breathing in the cool, still air, and feel the cave's story deep inside you: slow drips accumulate.

What stirred in you as you imagined this cavern? Capture here any feeling, memory, or idea that rose to the surface.

NOTICE WHAT STANDS OUT

Inside the cavern, what drew your attention?

- the subtle, echoing drips
- the cool, quiet air
- the hidden, secret feel of the cave
- the slow drip from above
- the rise of forms building below
- something else

Spend a moment with what most captivates you.

∼⁀ CONSIDER

1. These graceful formations began with simple drips accumulating over time. *What ongoing experiences in your estrangement have slowly shaped something new in you?* Put words to the shifts that have taken place and the strength that has grown in you.

2. Icicle-like stalactites begin with a single drop. *Can you think of any minor actions or attitudes you once brushed aside that you now see differently? What helped you recognize their impact? Can you take that recognition to other areas of your life in a way that benefits you?*

3. Stalagmites build upward from what falls. *What inner strengths, such as discernment, boundaries, or resilience, have been forming in you drop by drop? How might you acknowledge the slow, steady growth you've earned?*

4. Flowstone forms where water spreads and settles. *Where in your life have emotions pooled or become layered over time? What has become "hardened" in you, or simply preserved, for better or worse? What layers might you want to soften or honor?*

5. The beautiful cave formations look strong and grow more permanent over time. Still, they are delicate in places. *Where in your life do you feel both strong and sensitive? What kinds of moments touch those tender areas? How might you support yourself when those feelings surface?*

6. Sometimes, stalactites and stalagmites meet, becoming steady columns. *In your journey, where have understanding and experience met, forming new kinds of inner stability?*

SWEEPING THE SELF

As you go about your life, notice the slow accumulation that collects around you. Things like dust gathering, leaves or pebbles nudged into a runoff. Take a moment to clear or sweep one small area or a part of it. As you take this action, acknowledge what has built up in you while remembering that you can choose what stays, shifts, or no longer belongs.

eleven

WHEN WARM MEETS COLD

As the heat of summer cools into autumn, air temperatures drop more quickly than in dense bodies of water like ponds and lakes. So, cool air drifting across the water's surface gets warmed. Where warmth and coolness meet, the effect is "steam fog"—vapor that lifts and condenses into a soft rising mist.

Relax your eyes now, easing any tension between your brows. Allow your jaw to go slack and your shoulders to droop. Draw in a slow, deep breath through your nose. Exhale through your mouth with force.

Now, breathing easily, imagine ... an early morning walk near a lake. Sunlight slants in over eastern hills, highlighting a wispy film of steam that lifts off the water. The air is cool on your face and hands, but you know the lake holds the warmth of yesterday's sunlight. A swan glides through the vapor, looking almost magical as the swirling ribbons of steam embrace it.

You pause at the water's edge, aware of the softest of lapping at your feet. A faint earthy scent reaches your senses as the lake releases a bit of its warmth. Before you, the foggy mist curls and lifts, revealing shimmering patches of water, sparkling in the morning sun. You stand there for a moment, awed as the lake joins the day. When a hawk's long cry pierces the air, you turn and continue walking the lake's shore path, greeting the day yourself.

What sensation, thought, memory, or idea arose as you stood at the water's edge? Make a note.

⟞⟝ NOTICE WHAT STANDS OUT

As you imagine standing at the edge of the lake, notice what draws you in.

- the wispy mist
- the feel of the cold air or warm sun
- the sunlight, sparkling on the water
- the swan, so graceful in its solitude
- or something else

Linger at the water's edge for a moment, giving attention to what calls you.

∼ REFLECT

1. Lakes hold warmth long after the air cools. In estrangement, many parents carry a similar emotional warmth: caring, hoping, or trying long past the point of mutual connection. *How does this metaphor reflect your own experience? What thoughts or feelings surface as you consider the "temperature difference" between the warmth you offered and the distance your adult child created?*

2. When warm water meets cool air, rising mist shows evidence of the exchange. *As you imagine this meeting, notice what appears for you—thoughts, emotions, or memories.* Some may pass through lightly. Others may linger. *What do you notice?*

3. Steam fog softens the hard line between water and air. *What dates or occasions fog the reality of your relationship and your acceptance of what is beyond your power? Where in your healing does clarity become blurred by habit, hope, or fear? What helps clear the fog?*

4. As the day's light and warmth strengthen, the vapor's filmy hold recedes. The lake is revealed: strong, present, and gently moving. *When in your life have you experienced a similar independence? What support, activity, or self-respecting attitudes have thinned away emotional fog? What can you do or seek more of to see clearly and resume your own life rhythm?*

5. The lake joins the day, each at its own rhythm. *How can you move at your own pace, even when you're offered advice or you catch yourself comparing your healing to someone else's? In what ways might you respond to contact from or news about your estranged one in accord with what's right for you? How might you honor yourself rather than reacting to someone else's temperature or timeline?*

CHOOSING YOUR TEMPERATURE

Whenever you wash your hands, notice the temperature of the water. *Is it cool? Warm? Changing as you adjust the tap?* Pause and remind yourself: *you get to choose your temperature.* You can respond according to your own comfort.

twelve

THE LIGHT YOU CARRY

A bare flame flickers with the slightest breeze and, with stronger wind, is perhaps extinguished. Held in the shelter of a lantern, a flame remains strong. Warmth gathers within the enclosure, shielded from wind, and given fuel, allows a tiny flame to burn reliably. In darkness, its glow appears brighter, making a vulnerable flame unexpectedly luminous. Cold air, dense with oxygen, can feed a flame and brighten it. Yet cold can also steal heat and weaken it if protection is thin or fuel runs low. A flame needs shelter and tending. So do parents in the chilling draft of an adult child's abuse or rejection.

Take in a long, calming breath ... and let it go. Draw in another, allowing your shoulders to soften and your jaw to release. As your breath settles into its natural rhythm, fully relax.

Now, imagine . . . you're walking along a quiet path at dusk. The last traces of daylight are slipping over the horizon, and the air has cooled. You carry a glass lantern with a wire frame. Inside, a small flame burns.

As the air darkens into velvety night, a breeze ruffles your hair and tugs at your sleeves. Instinctively, you check the flame. Protected within the lantern's glass, it shivers slightly, then rises again, glowing ever brighter in the deepening darkness. You hold the lantern ahead of you, its light like an extension of yourself as you step along. It casts layers of radiance on the path, and its soft glow encircles you—as if you, too, are held within its gentle protection.

You feel at ease as you walk, the lantern's warmth subtly radiating toward your hand on the wire grip. The flame is alive, moving with and belonging to you. Bright, resilient, strong.

A hoot owl sounds its call, and you pause a moment, embraced in the circle of light. Another owl hoots its reply, and you lower the lamp, darkness blanketing all but a tiny sphere of light near your feet. Above you, stars shine from the veil of the sky, and you imagine them as lanterns held by others on equally dark paths. A cool breeze whistles down, and the flame in your lantern flickers. You raise it higher, cupping the opening with your palm. You're heartened by how the flame rights itself and embraces you in light once again. You step forward, shining your light on the path. You know the way.

What comes to mind when you imagine this? Write a few thoughts or feelings.

∼୨ NOTICE WHAT STANDS OUT

As you linger with this scene, what calls to you?

- the owls
- the beauty of the night sky
- the glow around you
- the weight of the lamp in your hand
- something else

Pause and allow your imagination to further illuminate the scene and whatever draws your attention.

⟳ CONSIDER

1. Lanterns shield a small flame from wind and movement, allowing it to burn steadily even in harsh conditions. *What part of you—a quality, inner truth, or core value—has remained steady or even grown stronger despite what has happened?*

2. In deep darkness, a flame appears brighter and more defined be-
    cause the contrast sharpens its glow. *What dark moments or painful
    realizations have helped you see something in yourself, about someone
    else, or about life more clearly?*

3. A gentle breeze feeds oxygen to a flame, causing it to flicker but then rise taller and shine more vividly. *What challenges, criticisms, or emotional "winds" have perhaps felt threatening yet unexpectedly strengthened you? What do they reveal about your resilience now?*

4. A lantern's flame reflects off its glass panels, creating layers of light that move with each step. *Since this all began, what layers of strength, clarity, or self-understanding have emerged or grown stronger on your healing path? How do these new layers influence the choices you make for yourself now?*

5. When a lantern is lifted higher, its light expands, illuminating more of the path ahead. *What recent information, choices, or shifts in perspective have helped you "lift your light" and see your way forward with greater confidence or calm?*

6. Above you, stars shine like lanterns held by others on dark paths. *As you sit with that image, what do you notice about your own path right now?*

HOLD THE LIGHT

Close your eyes and picture your lantern with its steady flame. Bring to mind at least one quality in yourself that has stayed present through difficulty. Something that endures even when you have felt shaken. Name it. With one hand resting on your heart, acknowledge this part of you, the light you carry.

thirteen
AFTER THE FIRE

Without intervention, forests naturally fill in with dry branches, an understory of brittle vegetation, and thick layers of fallen leaves. This buildup becomes dangerous fuel. A single spark can ignite a wildfire that rages through and devours nearly everything in its path. In contrast, a controlled burn is set with care, clearing the crowded forest floor and opening the canopy to allow in pockets of light. Heat coaxes certain long-dormant seeds to finally release, some of which have waited years beneath the soil. Other seeds, carried in by wind or leftover from a time of flourishing, sprout quickly in the changed landscape. Whether wildly fierce or intentionally set and controlled, fire can uncover what's hidden and make room for something new to grow.

Rest your hands in your lap and take a long breath in. Audibly sigh with your out-breath. Roll your shoulders and relax.

Now, imagine ... you're on a forest path in an area recently shaped by fire. A faint char smell lingers in the crisp morning air. All around you, ancient oaks with blackened trunks have sprouted wreaths of new greenery near the ground, the bright leaves both cheerful and defiant. A soft breeze brings a descent of woodpeckers near, and their jerky flight draws your attention upward as they fly on. Overhead, clusters of leaves sprout on scorched limbs. Like tiny bells, the new leaves tremble in the wind.

Touched by the signs of life, you walk on to a clearing. The ground is dark, the soil bare, the ashen remains of old growth scattered like shadows. You pause, taking in the stark scene. Then a blue-gray moth drifts across your path. You follow its flitting movement as it dips close to the earth and alights on a tiny violet colored flower. You smile, suddenly noticing a scattering of more slender shoots that have pierced the ash. These sprouts of unfolding life promise a meadow but were easily overlooked until the flicker of wings guided your gaze.

In this burned place, new life is making its way.

What feelings, thoughts, or memories come to mind? Spend a moment writing whatever the image has stirred.

◠◡ NOTICE WHAT STANDS OUT

Which part of this landscape holds your attention?

- the blackened oaks sprouting new growth
- the woodpeckers
- the leaves trembling like bells
- the bare soil in the clearing
- the moth's flitting
- the greenery rising through ash
- something else

Let yourself linger where your imagination is led. Sometimes the smallest detail carries a message of insight.

REFLECT

1. Long-dormant seeds crack open when exposed to heat, allowing for new beginnings. *What seeds of meaning, past dreams, or forgotten talents or skills has this period of anguish renewed in you?*

2. Amid a busy life, we sometimes overlook things that become visible in stillness. *What do you notice now—about yourself, life in general, others— that you didn't notice, or didn't have the time or space to ponder before?*

3. Fire clears away the tangled understory that would otherwise suppress new growth. *What emotional "understory" has estrangement brought to the surface or even cleared?* Perhaps old hurts, expectations, guilt, or long-avoided truths. *How might you continue to use a "controlled burn" to clear your path forward?*

4. Fire opens the forest canopy, allowing light to reach places that were long in shadow. *What has become clearer to you now that certain roles, pressures, or illusions have burned away?*

5. Some plants sprout quickly in ash-rich soil, drawing strength from elements fire has returned to the earth. *What strengths, insights, or capacities have begun to emerge in you—however small—that might not have appeared without this painful upheaval? How can you nurture these?*

WITNESSING RENEWAL

Think of one or more people, past or present, who experienced profound, life-changing upheaval. This could be:

- someone you personally know
- a public figure or historical person you admire
- a writer, artist, or thinker whose story has stayed with you

Take a moment to reflect upon what you know of their journey. What did they clear away, rebuild, or re-choose after their own "fire"? Which of their qualities do you find meaningful or strengthening?

As you reflect, notice what resonates with you personally. Can you draw any parallels? Sometimes another person's resilience helps illuminate yours.

If you'd like, write their name(s) below and note one or two qualities that stand out.

fourteen

YOUR HEARTH GLOWS

cross cultures and centuries, before central heating, families tended fire daily, banking embers, stirring coals, and feeding in small pieces of wood to keep it alive. The hearth was the center of the home. A well-kept hearth ensured warmth, safety, and a place to gather. Even when flames died away, the fire's glow persisted for hours beneath the ash, ready to rise into flames again with a breath and a stir. In long winters, the hearth was a lifeline.

Take in a long, steadying breath ... and let it go. Draw in another breath and, upon exhale, let your shoulders drop and your jaw slacken. Allow your breath to settle into its natural rhythm, letting your body soften and your mind rest.

Now, imagine ... your car has stalled. You're out of gas on a bitter winter afternoon, about four blocks from home. You managed to coast safely to the side of the road. Still, a flush of embarrassment rises. How could you let your car run out of gas? *Too much stress. Too much on your mind.* You glance around, glad no one's out, but feeling so very alone. Your chest tightens at the thought.

You unlock your phone and the screen lights, but the thought of explaining to someone keeps you from calling for help. The last thing you need is more judgment. You'll walk. You're close enough. You pop open the door and get out, your breath swirling in pale, fleeting clouds. Pulling your coat tight, you step to the gravelly shoulder. The cold settles quickly into your fingers, and you shove your hands into your pockets, wishing you'd brought gloves. A cutting wind slices across your nose and cheeks. You should have worn a hat too.

Your footsteps land with a steady *crunch-crunch-crunch* against the winter silence as you walk beneath barren trees, their limbs like out-stretched bones against the stark gray sky. The landscape mirrors your life. You're alone, navigating a situation you didn't choose and can't control. And now this dumb mistake. You clear your throat and go on, trusting your legs to get you to safety.

Finally, you reach your home and turn up the walk in relief. You fumble for your key with cold-brittle fingers. This house you shaped with hard work and enduring love has held you through so many seasons. As you open the door, you feel the warmth of welcome, as if the place recognizes you, too. Once inside, you head straight for the hearth. A stir with the poker reveals last night's embers, still aglow. Relieved, you feed in bits of newspaper and watch the flame rise and catch. Then you add wood, and lean closer to warm your hands.

After a few moments in the safety of your home, with the warmth of the fire seeping in, you loosen your coat. Maybe your neighbor has a gas can. You can ask. You've been through so much lately. Everyone has run out of gas at some point, and you lent your gas can to your only child. You thought you'd get it back.

You stand, gazing for a moment at the framed photos resting on the mantle. What was once your whole world is held in those images, in the face that once adored you. You devoted so much of yourself. So much time and energy in the family you believed would last.

In the mirror above the photos, you catch a glimpse of your reflection. Exhausted, you step onto the hearth, the heat pleasant on your shins. You touch the lines forming an eleven between your brows. They never seem to relax these days. *Enough.* You look again at the photos, the fire near your shins now beginning to sting. You step back, thinking how quickly something wonderful can change.

Yet here you are. Home.

What comes to mind as you imagine this? Write a few thoughts or feelings now.

∼◦ NOTICE WHAT STANDS OUT

As you reflect upon this scene, what draws your attention?

- the feeling of embarrassment at running out of gas
- the biting cold
- the walk beneath bare branches
- the relief of finding embers, and the fire's warmth
- the photos on the mantle
- the glimpse of your weary self in the mirror
- something else

Linger with whatever detail draws you in.

⌒⌒ REFLECT

1. Just as bitter winter days can make everything seem more difficult, times of stress and heartache can cause a person to forget something basic. *When have you neglected something as fundamental as filling the car with gas? Can you relate to the feelings of embarrassment and isolation?*

2. Like the fire with its embers still alive in the ash, people are often more resilient than they feel or think they are. *In this difficult season, what "embers" have you found within yourself? How are you, or how can you, "stir" them more to life?*

3. Compassion softens the impact of cold. *These days, how are you offering yourself compassion both in your thinking and in your behavior? In what ways can you be kinder to yourself? How have your toughest experiences enhanced your ability to understand other people's struggles?*

4. Last night's fire holds heat that can be tended to new warmth. *How are you seeking or beginning to imagine a renewed "fire" within you? In what ways do you feel ready for new warmth and purpose?*

5. A warm home feels even warmer after a cold walk. Our perspective shifts once we're safe. *How can you imagine yourself as "home"? When you're safely inside your own life, what do you begin to see differently about your needs, your limits, or your direction?*

6. Consider past choices, old patterns, and what truly supports your well-being. *Going forward, what will you hold fast to? What can loosen its grip on you? What might need more time, space, or energy before you know how to best proceed?*

TEND YOUR HEARTH

Close your eyes and picture last night's embers resting under ash. Now, imagine what might be "embers" in your own life. Think of people, activities, practices, or places. Whatever brings you joy. Who or what still "glows" for you? Make a list here. Add more as they come to you in the future. Once you have your list started, turn to it often. Choose one or two from your list to start and make a practice of adding a bit of "fuel," even five minutes to tend to them. Do things such as touch base with a friend from the list—an email, text, or call. Or, see a movie, visit a nature trail—whatever you've listed. Over time and with your tending, embers will catch like in a warming fire.

fifteen

WHAT WON'T CATCH

Wet wood resists burning. Even with kindling, accelerants, and effort, it produces more smoke than flame. In many regions, scheduled "burn days" when winds are calm allow residents an efficient clean-up method with minimal danger of fire risk. The downside is that the best time to trim trees is in winter, when they're more dormant and the birds have left their nests. But freshly cut wood must rest, dry, and season before it burns well. Until it's ready, no amount of tending will make it catch.

Take in a slow breath ... and release it. Draw in another, letting your shoulders soften and your jaw relax. As your breath settles naturally, allow your mind to still.

Now, imagine ... you're raking leaves on a crisp fall day when you smell it—the suffocating stench of smoke. You lean your rake against a tree and turn to see smoke drifting uphill on the breeze. You step toward the wire deer fencing that separates your top-of-the-hill land from the property below and see the source. The new neighbor is taking advantage of a county burn day.

You cup your hand over your nose and mouth as gray smoke billows from the brush pile he's trying to ignite. Even from a distance, you hear his cough. You watch as he splashes what looks like lighter fluid onto the pile, strikes a match, and tosses it in. Almost instantly, flames flare up. They collapse just as quickly. He tries again ... and again, with the same results: a brief flash, then a choking cloud. The wood he's using is freshly cut. *Too wet to catch.*

You consider calling down to him but stop yourself. You've been in his shoes. When you moved from the city like he recently did, you discovered how much you didn't know: wet wood refuses to burn, fresh brush smolders, and some things take time. You recall those early days of learning. There was always something to clear or chop or stack.

Feeling tenderness for your neighbor, you turn toward the house. He'll learn the rhythms of this place. Everyone does.

Inside, your fireplace glows. The seasoned wood you stacked months ago—spaced for air flow, protected from rain, dried by sun— cleanly burns. You stand and watch the fire for a moment, feeling its warmth. You didn't get here overnight.

After imagining yourself in this moment, where do your thoughts and feelings go?

∽ NOTICE WHAT STANDS OUT

As you linger with this scene, what draws your attention?

- the first smell of smoke
- the gray plumes drifting uphill
- the wet wood that won't catch
- the brief flare and quick collapse of flame
- your tenderness in recognizing your neighbor's struggle
- your steady fire burning inside
- something else

Pause to linger with whatever catches your attention.

∼ CONSIDER

1. Smoke clouds everything. *In your estrangement, what "smoke" once blurred your judgment? What did you interpret as personal failure that you see differently now?*

2. Cut wood refuses to burn until it has dried and rested. *What parts of you feel like they are still "seasoning," as in settling, lightening up, or changing in ways that can't be rushed?*

3. Trying to force wet wood to light creates more smoke. *Where might stepping back, rather than pushing harder, be wiser, safer, or more protective of your well-being?*

4. Some relationships or expectations turn out to be "wet wood." *Which efforts, hopes, or patterns have shown you that conditions just aren't quite right at this time?*

5. Dry, seasoned wood burns well. *What people, practices, or daily rhythms feel like good fuel for your life at this point?*

6. Burn days exist for a reason. *If you honored your own best times to take action, when would those be? When is it wiser for you to rest or wait?*

SORTING THE WOODPILE

Close your eyes and imagine returning to a cozy, well-tended hearth. Brick or stone. A place to sit. Embers glowing or with a steady flame. *It's yours.*

Now think about your life as a stack of wood resting near the hearth. Some pieces are wet with hurt, grief, or uncertainty. Some pieces are in the midst of seasoning. They're drying out and lightening up—not ready but on their way. And some pieces are ready now. They're dry and light, primed to provide warmth without filling your life with smoke.

On the lines on the next page are labels for three lists:

- *Wet wood.* Here's where you'll stack what still creates confusion.

- *Seasoning wood.* List here what needs time, space, or clarity, but is beginning to feel possible.

- *Ready wood.* Name what's pleasingly warm and supports your life. People, pets, activities, etc.

Don't stress over how many you list. Just get started. This week, notice what's "ready wood," and tend to it, even in a small way. Use the lines to write a little about what you did, and what you might try next. Additionally, if something you listed under any label surprised you or caused distress, take a little time to journal about it. *Why do you feel the way you do? How much control do you have over the item? Is it something you can let rest for now?*

WET WOOD

SEASONING WOOD

READY WOOD

sixteen

THE WIND THAT LIFTS YOU

Many birds partner with the wind, floating through the wide blue sky with ease. Some hawks ascend on rising thermal air currents, circling higher with just a few wingbeats. Others, like turkey vultures, may glide low, riding weaker shifting winds that thread through woodland trees and over hillsides. Each bird finds its own current, leaning into what lifts, guides, or carries it forward.

Take in a slow, steady breath ... and let it go. Draw in another, allowing your shoulders to drop and your face to relax. As your breath settles into its natural rhythm, let your chest soften and your mind begin to quiet.

Now, imagine ... a string of tense texts has left you frustrated, your chest and jaw feeling tight. Instinctively, you head outdoors where a wide swath of blue sky blankets the world. A warm breeze brushes your skin, and you tilt your face upward to relish its calming touch.

Your gaze catches two hawks high above, circling in wide arcs. Their flight is graceful and repeating, climbing higher as their invisible paths intersect and drift apart. Their wing beats are scarce, brief effort between long stretches of floating on air.

Your arms fall to your sides. A shadow passes by, and you follow it to its source: a turkey vulture, sweeping low over the rooftop and down over the hill, tilting its broad, dark wings to steer. You watch in astonishment as it threads itself, inches-close, between the branches of ancient heritage oaks, unfazed by the shifting wind.

Two types of birds in the same sky, using existing winds in different ways. The texts cross your mind again, this time feeling less important, like distant wind that doesn't stir you. You don't have to react or brace yourself. You can choose a different current, gliding on what carries you forward: nature, routines that add meaning, and whatever brings you joy.

What sensations, thoughts, or memories arose for you as you immersed yourself in this scene?

∽ NOTICE WHAT STANDS OUT

As you linger with this scene, what draws your attention?

- the circling hawks high above
- the turkey vulture weaving through the oaks
- the caress of the breeze on your face
- the wide blue sky
- something else

Take a moment. Let your attention rest on what calls to you.

⌒୭ REFLECT

1. Hawks conserve energy by circling on warm updrafts that help them gain altitude with little effort. *When you've felt weighted down, what "natural lifts," such as supportive environments, optimism, or simple routines, have helped you rise?*

2. Turkey vultures often glide at lower altitudes by using weak updrafts, such as those coming off trees. *What are the sources of support in your life that aren't necessarily big or dramatic but steady you in difficult times?*

3. At lower altitudes, turkey vultures tilt and rock, adjusting to the terrain as they slip through tight spaces such as through the branches of closely growing trees. *What small adjustments have you made to your routines, responses to other people, or your environment, that have helped you move through emotionally tight terrain?*

4. Birds can conserve energy by using wind rather than flapping their wings harder. *Where might less effort support your well-being? What does "using the wind" look like for you?*

5. Birds can shift altitude with purpose: flying low reveals details; rising higher reveals patterns that aren't visible from the ground. *Where in your healing have you begun to see a larger pattern, or notice truths that were hidden when you were closer to the pain?*

6. Even in shifting winds, birds trust their wings to carry them. *What can you trust in yourself right now? How can you lean into these inner strengths more fully?*

RIDING THE WIND

As you move through your days, notice any moments when tension rises—perhaps after an interaction, a thought, or an unexpected reminder. Pause briefly and offer yourself compassion. Life is not always straightforward or easy.

Ask yourself: *What feels like a supportive current for me right now?*

It might be a familiar routine, a place you trust, a steady breath, or a shift in focus. Let yourself lean into what carries you, even in a small way, and continue on.

Later, during quiet time, consider what ongoing practices might help you reduce effort. Things like:

- delaying a response
- shortening a task
- choosing a familiar comfort instead of a "should"
- stepping outside, stretching, or resting instead of powering through

Choose one or two to follow-through on and, as you do, say or think: *You don't have to flap harder. You can let the wind help.*

Note here what you'll try and the results.

seventeen

WHEN LIGHT APPEARS

ouseplants adapt to their environment by adjusting their growth. When nourishing resources are limited, plants may lean toward light, drop leaves to conserve energy, or grow more slowly until conditions change.

Settle into a position that feels easy and comfortable. After a cleansing breath, feel what's supporting your body. Relax into the moment. There's nowhere else you need to be.

Now, imagine ... it's late afternoon, and weak winter light slants through a tiny opening in the drapes at the sliding glass door. As if waking from a long sleep, you look around your living room. It's a bit unkempt after all you've been through lately, but it's still a place you love.

Across the room, a tall houseplant you've had for years leans sharply toward the narrow shaft of sunlight. How long has it been since you last opened those drapes? Months have passed. A winter before the real one. With a frown over so much lost time, you draw the drapes fully open.

You blink at the sudden light spilling in and notice a few dried leaves that have fallen from your plant. You gather them into the pocket of your robe and touch a glossy, dark green leaf near the top of your long-lived companion—leaning, yes, but still strong.

Then you spot a single trailing vine, long and bare, stretching down from the bookshelf pot in its search for light. The ropey stem looks lifeless at first, but a tiny new leaf is unfurling at the very tip. Your head tilts in response, acknowledging its hopeful persistence. Despite your neglect, the plant found light.

You lift the vine and rest it on the drapery rod for now. A swell of gratitude rises in your throat. Your neglected plants hold a lot of life. So do you.

What thoughts, memories, or feelings come to you? Take a moment to reflect on what rises.

∽ NOTICE WHAT STANDS OUT

As the scene lingers in your imagination, what is prominent?

- the narrow band of winter light
- the leaning, long-lived houseplant
- the fallen leaves you gather and pocket
- the bare vine, stretching
- the tiny new leaf unfurling
- the opened drapes and light spilling in
- something else

Rest a moment with whatever draws you in.

⟋⟍ CONSIDER

1. A room can be unkempt and still hold you in warmth and familiarity. *What parts of yourself or your life feel imperfect yet still offer comfort or a sense of "home" to you?*

2. When overwhelmed, many people withdraw from their own needs without realizing. *Where have you recently noticed signs of self-neglect? What efforts at tending might help you reconnect with yourself?*

3. Opening the drapes changes the whole room; one small shift sheds light. *What small action, boundary, or change in attention has recently opened something in you (or could)?*

4. Renewal is often sparked by the tiniest beginnings, like the single shaft of sunlight through the drapes. *What new growth, insight, strength, interest, or possibility has begun to emerge in you, no matter how small?*

5. Houseplants show their needs in subtle ways such as leaning, stretching, or dropping leaves. *When you've needed support, how have you signaled this, even subtly? Who has noticed, and who might you consider letting in more clearly?*

LIGHT IN NARROW PLACES

Make a practice of noticing "shafts of light" that appear in your life. Look for and savor anything that brings relief, a hint of comfort, or warmth. By noticing a moment of wonder, a kind interaction, or the satisfaction of completing a task, you train yourself to be more attuned to the moments that infuse life with hope and joy. Take notice. Write here what you find and how it helped. Doodle if you'd like.

eighteen

YOUR CLOUDSCAPE

Clouds form when water vapor cools and condenses around tiny particles in the air, creating ever-shifting shapes that drift across the sky. Wind currents sculpt their edges, sunlight adds dimension, and our pattern-seeking brains interpret the forms as animals, faces, or familiar scenes. Though they may appear heavy or defined, clouds are mostly air—structures that look solid but are constantly changing.

Soften your gaze now. Breathe naturally, aware of the air coming in and going out in an easy rhythm. Imagine the space between your lungs, around your organs, and all inside you. You're more space than you are matter.

Now, imagine ... you've stepped outside on a startlingly beautiful day that you wish you could better enjoy. The sky is awash in deep blue.

Puffy white clouds drift lazily on a gentle breeze. Lovely, but barely registered beyond the fog of pain and anger alive in your mind. Thoughts crowd in: what was said on the phone recently, the tone of voice that's becoming familiar, and the dreadful worry because you haven't spoken since. *Is everything okay?*

Your mind centers on what you replied, how you said the words, and the way you wish for the old days when a hurt or a tantrum could be met with a hug, and all would be okay. It isn't like that now. You grit your teeth. Your arms close over your chest. After all that has happened, why do you even care? You made a deal with yourself that you wouldn't be the one to call. Not this time after so many other times you tried to fix an argument you don't understand.

The chaotic feelings pile in like storm fronts, and you feel sick. You sit down on the porch steps, elbows on your knees, and stare into space. A massive, bright cloud drifts overhead, barely noticed. Your thoughts are circling, tightening, pulling you inward.

Somewhere from beyond the fence, you hear a child's laughter, bright and bubbly, drifting on the breeze. The sound lands in your chest with a mix of warmth and ache, stirring a rush of memories—your childhood, your child's, perhaps even your grandchild's. For a heartbeat, you can't distinguish between sorrow or joy.

You look up, and the sky opens to you as if it has been waiting. A small, lopsided cloud breaks away from a larger formation. It slowly stretches and, for the briefest moment, looks like a dog wearing a party hat.

As quickly as it appeared, the hat is gone, and the dog unravels. The lilt of surprise it brought to you lingers. How absurdly simple that the heaviness you felt could dissolve away, as fleeting as a cloud reshaping on the breeze.

You lean back, letting your chest open toward the sun. More clouds drift by. What do you see? Perhaps one cloud looks vaguely like a teapot.

Another, a sleeping cat. None of them stay for long. They stretch, blur, dissolve, and re-form in ways you can't predict.

The breeze feels good on your sun-warmed skin. Nothing has been solved. All the pain and the questions remain—but they're farther away now. You stand and stretch, imagining yourself as light and free as a cloud reshaping.

Take a moment longer to expand this imagery in your mind's eye. What clouds take shape? What memories or thoughts come to mind?

⌒ NOTICE WHAT STANDS OUT

As you linger with this scene of sky and shifting clouds, what draws your attention?

- the blue sky opening above you
- a particular cloud shape
- the child's laughter
- the warmth of the sun
- the shift inside
- something else

Settle on what captures your attention, stirs emotion, or reminds you of something.

⌒๑ REFLECT

1. Clouds can appear heavy, ominous, or solid. Yet, they're only vapor. *What in your life has looked heavier or more threatening than it truly was once you stepped back or gained perspective?*

2. Clouds drift and reshape. *Where in your life are you beginning to release an old story, identity, or assumption that once felt fixed?*

3. Sometimes a small interruption—a sound, a memory, a moment of beauty—breaks through heavy thoughts and shifts your view. *What recent moment, however brief, helped you see something differently in your healing?*

4. Sometimes a change in perspective only occurs because we step outside ourselves, even briefly. *Where have you recently taken a small step out of your emotional isolation, and what did it open for you?* Also consider what you might try next, if anything.

5. Clouds shift in shape without holding to any single form. *Where are you beginning to allow yourself to change without defending those changes?*

LET THE SKY IN

Go outdoors (or to a window) and look up at the sky. No need to search for meaning or try to see anything specific. Just notice:

- the way the light shifts
- the movement of the clouds
- their colors and edges
- anything that softens, brightens, or changes

If a cloud briefly resembles something, register it without holding on.

Take a moment to write down at least one thing that eased your outlook—even briefly. A shift, a softening, a moment of unexpected perspective, or simply that you looked up.

Openness can be subtle practice. Even in painful seasons, small moments of light reach you when you let the sky in.

nineteen

WHAT GROWS?

Nutsedge is a persistent weed that frustrates even the most sea-soned gardeners. Its glossy green shoots look innocent enough, but beneath the surface lies a network of tiny nutlets—each one capable of sprouting when conditions allow. Pulling it up rarely works. The stem snaps off, leaving the vigorous nutlets intact underground. Digging deeper helps, but the interconnected network means some nutlets remain behind. Disturbing the soil can even awaken dormant ones. Gardeners say, "Once you have nutsedge, you'll always have nutsedge." This weed is one you learn to work with rather than always fight.

Let your shoulders drop, draw in a breath, and release it with a sigh. Breathing easily now, imagine settling into yourself the way untouched soil settles after rain.

Now, imagine ... you're outside on a cool morning, tending the garden area near your walkway. You've been working for a while, pulling weeds, shaking soil from their roots, and discarding them. You're glad to see rich, cleared earth alongside your flowering bushes again. Then you spot a familiar fountain of glossy green leaves on a sturdy shoot that's pushing up proudly on the other side of the walkway. *Not again.*

You remember the first time you saw it last spring, an intriguing tuft of green in the beds you were clearing alongside the curving cement path. The fountain shape looked special, and you thought it might be an exotic volunteer plant you could nurture. When you accidentally cut through it with your shovel as you were loosening the soil, you felt a pang of guilt. *Had you destroyed something promising?*

Later, you discovered its identity—nutsedge. A relentless weed that looks good at first but tries to take over. Nothing you did could change it.

Feeling defeated, you sit back in the soil, the chill from the damp earth penetrating the backside of your jeans. Ever since you learned its true nature, you've been tugging this stuff out whenever it shows up. And each time, you've hoped the tenacious weed wouldn't return. But there it is again, the spray of fibrous leaves rising in defiance as if to mock you.

On hands and knees now, you lean close to pinch its base and pull. The stem breaks off, of course, leaving roots and nutlets to sleep underground. Hopefully for a long nap this time.

The thought feels silly and you smile, not letting this darned weed get the best of you. It's nutsedge, doing what nutsedge does. For a moment, you stare at the small hole where the stalk was and resist the urge to pick at it. You know better. Disturbing it only gives it strength.

A breeze whispers over your forearm. A bird chirps from the maple tree. A ladybug flies by. It's a beautiful morning. You won't let nutsedge steal any more of your energy.

Your gaze shifts to what's thriving right now: dahlias in pink and orange and yellow, stately blue agapanthus, and striking red geraniums.

You pinch a silver-green leaf from the mound of sage you know will endure the coming summer heat, relishing its invigorating citrus-musk scent. The nutsedge isn't an intentional part of your garden but it does exist. When it comes back, it comes back. You'll deal with it.

You stand, pull off your gloves, and move toward the house. Forget the darned weeds. You'll get your camera while everything beautiful is in bloom.

Take a moment with this scene. *What comes to mind?*

NOTICE WHAT STANDS OUT

As you linger with this imagery, what draws your attention?

- the glossy green fountain of nutsedge leaves
- the sturdy stem
- the futility of the fight
- the thriving beauty of the plants nearby
- the realization that your energy can be conserved
- something else

Let your attention rest on whatever speaks to you.

⤬ CONSIDER

1. Some things have a way of resurfacing, no matter how carefully we tend the soil around them. *Where in your healing have you noticed something resurface repeatedly?*

2. At first glance, some things look hopeful or harmless, and only later do we understand their true nature. *Where have you experienced a shift in understanding that helped you release guilt, self-blame, or wishful thinking about someone's behavior?*

3. Disturbing the soil can awaken what's dormant. *Rather than fixing, explaining, or intervening, where might stepping back protect your peace or emotional energy right now?*

4. Some situations intensify the more you try to fix or respond to them. *What have you learned about when not to engage? How does that choice protect your well-being?*

5. Some problems arise from situations you didn't start or places you didn't expect and can't control. *What shifts in you when you stop taking responsibility for whatever didn't start with you?*

LET IT BE

Choose one situation, memory, or recurring emotional "weed" that pops up for you. Instead of trying to uproot it completely, take a gentler approach:

- Acknowledge its presence without reacting.
- Remind yourself that its reappearance doesn't mean you've failed. It's just part of the landscape.
- Name one thing worth tending today that nourishes your stability, joy, or calm.

Write down what you're choosing to "let be" right now, and what you'll tend instead.

twenty

ANOTHER WAY

Mountains are frequently known for their highest peak. The name gets printed on trail maps, carved into signposts, and talked about as *the* destination for hikers to reach. That leaves a whole system of intersecting trails beneath the summit: shaded switchbacks, creek-side meanders, ridge walks, and contemplative overlooks tucked around unexpected bends. Some of these side routes offer easier footing, more beauty, and a broader perspective than the steep, well-trodden push toward the top.

Take a slow inhale, as if drawing in cool morning air. Exhale gently, letting anything tight or braced release. Feel the ground supporting you with ease.

Now, imagine ... it's an early morning just after sunrise. The air is cool, and the sun's light soft as you check the laces on your hiking boots.

Satisfied, you stand at the trailhead, a feather of dread rising up your spine. For years, you've climbed the same steep trail to the summit—even though there's nothing much up there. An accomplishment. The mindful trophy of completing a task.

Standing at the familiar starting point, you feel the weight of obligation, perhaps even resentment. Still, you start upward. The path climbs quickly. Your legs know the rhythm well. A third of a mile up, you pause at the washer-sized boulder where you always stop to catch your breath. When you begin again, you notice the weathered sign marking a spur trail. *How many times have you been by this thing?* Dozens—yet you've never taken the turn and explored.

You force a smile as a loud group of hikers comes down the steep summit trail. Exhilarated from the swift descent, they're laughing, so engrossed in each other they barely nod to you as they pass, their footfalls pounding.

With glaring clarity, you realize you don't want to do the climb. *Is it worth the effort?* You're tired of all the work. At least for today. Maybe forever.

You turn onto the narrow side trail that leads around the ridge lined with scrub oak and brush. As you put one foot in front of the other on the level trail, your thoughts wander to your estranged child, and your familiar hope that more effort, another attempt or climb, might somehow fix the rift or bridge what has become an impasse.

The path grows rockier, and you pause, the surroundings quiet. The spur trail was marked, but where's it leading you? Massive boulder outcroppings loom in the distance. The morning sun highlights patches of golden lichen. It all looks so dry.

A thin breeze skitters up the ridge, and you notice a single-trek trail, like a deer line, heading down into a shady ravine. Curious, you step toward the trail's opening and hear a soft bubbling in the distance. You take one sloping step down, and then another on the gradually descending path increasingly shaded by large oaks. The sound of water hums louder as you follow the trail. The air cools, and where patches of sunlight stream in through the canopy, bright flowers—yellow, white, and red—appear like spots of cheer. Birds scratch about for bugs in the underbrush, their soft chirps contented as you pass. You feel yourself start to relax, the urgency of the usual climb unwinding in you like a loosened knot.

When you reach the water, you stop, scooting onto a flattish rock. As the water bubbles past, your gaze follows its flow to several low waterfalls and places where the water pools and foams. Glints of sunlight spark diamonds and rainbows on its surface.

This isn't the dramatic sweep the summit once offered, but that's changed too. Once a painterly canvas of hills, layered like shadows in the distance, there is now a sea of rooftops.

For several minutes, your thoughts meander, reaching several swift currents and then pooling into gentle, sparkling memories. Your throat thickening, you find yourself swiping at a tear. Here, you can hear yourself think. So different than the summit climb where every second seems to count and the anxious tug to keep moving blots out everything else.

With a mix of sadness and relief, you realize your relationship with the summit has reached an impasse. The peak you used to work so hard to reach no longer holds a reward.

You breathe deeply, feeling the cool, oxygen-rich air at this lower elevation fill your lungs. Maybe you'll never make the summit climb again. It's your choice.

You relax for a few more minutes, keenly aware of a bird's single-note call that echoes in the trees above the stream, and the varying colors and textures of the moss growing on wet stones. The shifting depths of green look lush and peaceful, growing together yet so different.

When you feel ready, you stand and begin the short climb back to the ridge trail. Making your way back, you move comfortably, the brightening sunlight soft on your face. You feel oddly satisfied, as if this quieter path were a peak of its own.

What thoughts, memories, or feelings come to you? Take a moment to reflect.

∿ NOTICE WHAT STANDS OUT

As you linger with this scene, what draws your attention?

- the weight you felt at the summit trailhead
- the weathered spur-trail sign
- the loud, descending hikers
- the moment you realized you didn't want to climb
- the sound of the creek
- the glints of sunlight on the water
- the feeling of relief at choosing a different path
- something else

Let your attention settle on whatever evokes emotion, insight, or resonance.

REFLECT

1. The summit that was once important to you doesn't hold the draw for you it used to. *Have you noticed a similar shift elsewhere in your life?*

2. You had passed the spur trail many times before yet ignored it as an option. *What gentler direction or clarity has come into view because you stopped pushing so hard?*

3. A different path brought relief, beauty, and a realization about choice. *Where have you recently taken a detour that brought unexpected ease or insight? Or where might you try such a detour?*

4. Hope can make us overlook what hurts. *When you reflect honestly, what things have you chosen to move past without naming them? What do you understand differently now?*

5. The creek you discovered offered space to hear yourself think. *In the forward journey after estrangement, in what areas of your life could you choose a quieter, more self-compassionate route over a steep habitual one?*

A DIFFERENT TURN

Think of one area of your life where you've been climbing the same familiar "summit trail." That could be an old behavioral pattern, a habitual response, hope you keep revisiting despite costs, or an effort that leaves you exhausted.

In the space below, draw a simple fork-in-the-path picture. Label one route "the usual way," and list what that route costs you emotionally, physically, or spiritually.

Then label the other route "a different turn." What might that gentler detour be like? It could involve setting a boundary you keep, spending more time and energy on yourself, or some other shift in focus. Perhaps there is fun along this route. Write a few thoughts about this new way forward and its benefits.

twenty-one

WHAT'S NEAR IS ENOUGH

Fog forms when moisture in the air condenses near the ground, creating low clouds that scatter light and reduce visibility. Nearby objects may appear sharper and more defined, while distant landmarks fade or are completely obscured.

Pause for a moment and allow your gaze to soften. Notice where your body is supported, and feel the air against your skin. Relax your shoulders and breathe naturally. Right now, you have nowhere to be and nothing else to do.

Now, imagine … you're walking with your dog on a familiar path early in the morning. Fog has settled in overnight, thick enough to soften the edges of everything around you. The ground beneath your feet is still visible, but the trail ahead dissolves after a short distance.

Your dog trots slightly ahead, alert and curious, her nose low to the ground. You can see the shape of her back, the steady rhythm of her tail swaying as she moves. She's close enough that you feel comfortable letting the leash out a little more. As she takes up the slack, you walk faster, not as certain as she is about walking into what you can't yet see. You look around. The fog lends a magical feeling to the landscape. The soupy backdrop sharpens what's close to you. Even so, the lack of visibility farther ahead is unsettling. You've been here many times. You know where you're going. The path at your feet and just ahead clears as you move through it.

A scuttering sound shifts in the fog, and your grip tightens on the leash. Was that a bird? Or ...something else? Your dog pauses, ears pricked, then relaxes and pulls forward, taking up the slack again. Her outline thins as she steps into the denser fog and is swallowed by it.

Your breath catches but you have hold of the leash. The gentle pull assures you she's still with you, moving steadily along. You slow your pace, noticing what's clearly visible: the texture of the path beneath your boots, the dewdrops clinging to the grass at the trail's edge, the rough bark of a tree, and the shape of its narrow leaves, the dark channel running down the center of each. The air is cool and moist, your footfalls almost silent on the damp ground.

You glance back and see the path dissolving behind you, too. The fog is close, becoming familiar as you move along. Maybe even protective.

After a few more steps, the leash slackens a bit. Your dog's shape redefines. She glances back briefly, her tail wagging once, as if to say: *I'm here.*

The fog hasn't lifted, but for now, you know the way. What's near is enough.

⟢ Take a moment to consider memories or thoughts that arise from this passage. Write a few notes.

∽ NOTICE WHAT STANDS OUT

As you reflect on the scene, what draws you in?

- the uncertainty of not seeing clearly what's ahead
- the magical, protective feel of the fog
- the dog's independence—and devotion
- the moment of fear
- the obscured yet familiar trail
- something else entirely

Spend a few moments allowing these images to settle and, perhaps, spark contemplation.

⟿ CONSIDER

1. Fog reduces distant visibility but brings what's close into sharper focus. *In this season of your life, what feels unclear or hidden? What's right in front of you, deserving your attention or care?*

2. Even when the path ahead is uncertain, frequently we still "know the way." *Without overthinking, in what ways do you already sense your way forward?*

3. In fog, forward movement can require trust in yourself and what remains familiar. *Where in your healing are you learning to rely on what you know, even without seeing the whole picture?*

4. Fog can make potential hazards harder to assess. *What has helped you distinguish between real danger and the discomfort of not knowing what's ahead?*

5. While fog can be disorienting, it can also feel protective. *Where might it be acceptable, or even wise, for you to let some things remain out of view for now?*

WHAT YOU KNOW

Take a moment to notice what in your life is familiar, comfortable, steady, or known. Consider:

- routines you've settled into
- decisions you've made
- values you no longer question
- ways you've handled uncertain situations before

Where don't you need to push? Where do you trust yourself? Write out a few thoughts. Let yourself rest in what's solid.

twenty-two

HIGHER GROUND

When heavy rain falls in a short period of time, water levels rise. A pond can spread beyond its usual edge. Shorelines soften. Objects near the water are submerged. Footpaths disappear. Over time, conditions around a body of water can change, which complicates capacity. Reedy areas thicken. Sediment builds. Drainage shifts. Water flow slows down or gets redirected. Boundaries, benches, and pathways established long ago may no longer sit where the water stays contained. The structure remains but the environment has changed.

Pause with intention. Let your shoulders drop and your jaw slacken. Notice the weight of your body and where it's supported. Draw in a slow, steady breath ... and release it with an audible sigh. You're here now. There is nowhere else you need to be.

Now imagine ... you're standing at the top of the gentle slope that leads down to the small nature sanctuary's pond. Its far side is thick with reeds where the red-winged blackbirds frolic, but today no birds are present. The air is still. After yesterday's rain, the bench where you often sit listening to the birds' twanging calls stands in a puddle. The path around the entire pond is submerged.

Weeks may pass before the shoreline is dry enough to safely meander again. You know from unfortunate experience how slippery the mud there can be. The bench, placed there long ago, won't be accessible. You pause, taking it all in. Oh, how you love to walk the entire greenspace, snapping nature pictures as the sun warms your back. And then you sit and gaze at the sky's reflection in the glassy water. Those are carefree days.

Oh well. It's this way every year. The rainstorms arrive with pummeling might. The pond's edges blur as the murky water spreads beyond the banks. Now that you've learned the pattern, you've adopted your own. Each rainy season, you arrive with optimistic curiosity and see what you expected even while you still dare to hope. You quickly accept the circumstances. It's all familiar now. The weather, the pond ... they behave how they do.

The bench is there and sturdy, but you won't brave the wet shoes, soaked clothes, and unstable footing like you used to. Today, it's too close to the edge.

You stand back, surveying the quiet, dumped-upon scene. You'll tread the dry path up here above the pond. Last year, they laid a cement path that leads to a gazebo on an even higher rise. On these days, you're safer up here, above the flood zone.

∿ NOTICE WHAT STANDS OUT

As you linger with the scene, what stands out?

- the overflowing pond
- the bench
- the higher, dry path
- the feeling of standing back
- something else

Let your attention rest on whatever draws you. What might this mean?

⁓ REFLECT

1. When conditions shift, water levels rise, redirect, and recede. *As you imagined the pond scene, what felt familiar to your life right now?*

2. Structures placed near water may remain sound even when conditions make them inaccessible or inadequate. *What might the bench represent for you? What in yourself or your life, at times, is inaccessible or prudent to avoid?*

3. With experience comes the recognition of patterns and wiser responses. *How did it feel to imagine choosing not to risk approaching the bench today? What emotions, bodily sensations, or thoughts arise from the choice?*

4. Stepping back from an edge can reduce risk, even if you still long for the "bench." *Where in your life are you practicing discernment that keeps you from harm's way?*

5. Predictable cycles often carry both realism and hope. *When you approach familiar emotional seasons with "optimistic curiosity," what do you notice has changed in you over time?*

6. Relief can arise even if circumstances remain unresolved. *If a sense of relief appeared anywhere in this reflection, how did you respond?*

WHERE TO STAND

Think about the next time you might expect emotional "high water." Without judging the situation, determine:

- *Where is your edge?*

- *Where is your higher ground?*

- *Where do you feel safe?*

Write down at least one place, whether physical, emotional, or relational, where you can stand and feel grounded during that time.

WHERE YOU STAND: INTEGRATING WHAT YOU'VE NOTICED

As you've moved through the scenes within these pages, you've paused to contemplate whatever emerged for you. Your persistence illustrates your determination to live a meaningful life, even when it didn't unfold as you once imagined. *Well done.*

By immersing yourself in this imagery, you've entered the world of your strengths and vulnerabilities indirectly, without the pressure of confrontation. Along the way, you may have identified patterns within yourself and your life. Some reflections likely felt familiar. Others may have caught you off guard.

Estrangement has a way of interrupting life's natural rhythm, pulling the past into the present, and forcing decisions without certainty. The harsh light of a sudden rift can be unsettling yet also clarifying. You're asked to live with unanswered questions while still caring for yourself, other loved ones, and your continuing life.

Because estrangement rarely reaches a clean conclusion, this book doesn't try to force one. Instead, this is a chance to locate yourself in your ongoing story. With this final entry, I invite you to accept yourself wherever you stand.

Take a few moments to reflect upon your journey so far. At one point, you stood in shock, confusion, or self-doubt. You searched for explanations, replayed conversations, and perhaps took on responsibility that wasn't yours to shoulder. Even now, months or perhaps many years beyond the initial break, you still occasionally experience a flash of disbelief when reality strikes.

Yet you also notice your growing capacity to turn to and appreciate the beauty and kindness that still exist. You can lean into what's uplifting and nurture a sense of awe and gratitude for a life that shines forward despite the hurt.

WHERE DO YOU STAND?

Pause for a moment. Notice what comes to mind. Be aware of your body and how it feels right now. Feel free to express what arises—or simply sit with this.

NOTICE WHAT RESONATED

Below is a list of entries with short summaries. This isn't meant as a set of lessons so much as a completed itinerary—a traveled journey. You visited some places briefly and others more deeply. As you read through these titles and descriptions, put a checkmark or draw a star next to any entries that were especially meaningful to you. Circle ones you might want to return to.

1. YOUR SACRED FOUNTAIN

A quiet courtyard fountain invites awareness of emotional flow, depletion, and renewal, offering a gentle return to yourself when you feel dry, stalled, or disconnected.

2. YOUR HIDDEN FOREST

A damp woodland path and mushroom clusters reveal inner transformation. Emotional material is being processed and integrated, preparing and supporting you for what comes next in your life.

3. YOUR HEART'S RESPONSE

A sudden hailstorm reflects how protective responses are shaped by repeated emotional turbulence—and how softening can begin.

4. LIGHT IN A LOW PLACE

A rain-filled puddle on a familiar path reveals how even low or stagnant emotional places can reflect meaning, light, and unexpected nourishment.

5. WITHIN THE WAVES

While you stand at the ocean's edge, the rhythmic waves echo your emotional cycles, endurance, and what you've gathered: insight, strength, clarity.

6. SOLID GROUND

An earthquake and its possible aftershocks mirror emotional rupture, shaken nerves, and altered expectations, inviting reflection on what has shifted, what remains stable, and how you can regain your footing.

7. WHAT'S LEFT BEHIND

Rocky tidepools at low tide mirror the vulnerability, adaptation, and resilience that can naturally occur for you during unsettled seasons.

8. WHERE PRESSURE FINDS A PATH

Hot springs and steam vents illustrate healthy emotional release.

9. YOUR INNER WELL

A rustic well in a parched landscape reconnects you with your enduring inner resources.

10. WHERE DROPS TAKE SHAPE

Deep in the hidden chambers of a cave, slow mineral drips shape a delicate yet enduring inner strength over time.

11. WHEN WARM MEETS COLD

A misty lake at dawn reflects the emotional fog that forms when lingering warmth from a long-held bond meets separation. Clarity gradually returns.

12. THE LIGHT YOU CARRY

A lantern carried in darkness reflects core qualities that can brighten under strain.

13. AFTER THE FIRE

A forest shaped by fire invites you to notice what becomes visible, possible, or newly alive once the landscape has changed.

14. YOUR HEARTH GLOWS

A cold walk home and rekindled embers explore self-compassion, exhaustion, and the resilience that remains even when you feel depleted.

15. WHAT WON'T CATCH

Wet wood and a smoky burn pile reflect efforts that cannot yet take hold, offering permission to step back, wait, and conserve emotional energy.

16. THE WIND THAT LIFTS YOU

Hawks and vultures riding air currents reflect different forms of support—and the freedom to choose what's right for you now.

17. WHEN LIGHT APPEARS

In a dimly lit room, houseplants reveal self-neglect ... and the will to adapt.

18. YOUR CLOUDSCAPE

Drifting clouds mirror shifting thoughts and emotions, opening brief moments of emotional space and perspective.

19. WHAT GROWS?

A garden with reappearing weeds reflects emotional patterns that resurface over time, and the maturity to respond with wisdom rather than intensity.

20. ANOTHER WAY

On a mountain trail that once held meaning, a previously overlooked detour invites an alternate way forward—one that releases obligation and unnecessary effort.

21. WHAT'S NEAR IS ENOUGH

A foggy morning walk with a dog treads the tension between uncertainty and trust.

22. HIGHER GROUND

When familiar high-water seasons flood the pond and the path disappears, insight shaped by experience keeps you on safer footing, on higher ground.

Just as your life and history are unique, there is no absolute pattern here. You may have moved through the reflections as presented, skipped around, or lingered and repeated where you felt the need. Some reflections may have spoken loudly or merely whispered. Some will merit a future revisit in a different life season or as familiar cycles continue to engage you. You can always come back to those entries.

As you move forward, the years add wisdom and growth through experiences that tax or nurture. Life contains many landscapes. Grief can include hope. Love can include sorrow. Problems don't always resolve. Life doesn't always come to a tidy conclusion.

Ahead, your days will continue to require a mix of your discernment, adjustment, and self-trust. At times, old feelings may resurface, bringing questions you feel compelled to revisit. These might even include questions you thought you had set down once and for all. Be kind to yourself. You're moving through layers—more aware, and with the gentle compassion you've earned.

Now ... feel your body where you are. Notice whatever is supporting you. Feel your breath slow and easy, moving at its natural pace.

This is where you stand.

Right here and now. There's no need to justify or explain. You stand here in self-compassion, confident that love doesn't require you to sacrifice your safety or sense of self.

Whatever comes—contact, distance, words or silence—you can orient yourself on your own path, recognizing what's real, and starting fresh as needed.

The End.   The Beginning.   The In-Between.

Estrangement often places us in more than one of these at once.

⟲ CONSIDER

- *Where do you stand today?*
- *What feels complete, even partially?*
- **What are you allowing to remain unresolved, at least for now?**

Take a few restful minutes to respond in whatever way feels natural.
Write, doodle, or simply think about where you stand.

ABOUT THE AUTHOR

SHERI MCGREGOR is an author and life coach who has worked with parents of estranged adult children since 2013. Her award-winning *Done With The Crying* series has supported readers around the world, offering practical guidance and compassionate perspective while helping parents move forward and rebuild meaningful lives beyond estrangement. Her 2025 book, *Rumination Remedies: A Workbook to Free Your Mind from Worry, Regret, and Racing Thoughts*, was named a Publisher's Weekly BookLife Prize quarter finalist and expands her work in helping readers understand and ease patterns of the mind. Her work has also been published internationally, including in translation.

Sheri holds a Master's Degree in Human Behavior and has more than two decades of experience as a life coach. She continues to deepen her work through advanced training and certifications in brain-based coaching, the neuroscience of change, and aging-related wellness.

Her writing has appeared in a wide range of publications, reflecting a lifelong interest in both human behavior and everyday life.

Learn more at **www.RejectedParents.net**, where she offers resources, a supportive membership community, and ongoing programs for parents of estranged adult children.

EXPLORE MORE FROM SHERI McGREGOR

Done With The Crying: Help and Healing for Mothers of Estranged Adult Children
ISBN—print: 978-0997352207; e-book: 978-0997352214
Over 93,000 copies in circulation.
Winner: *Living Now Book Award*
Also available as a Tantor Media audiobook and
a Russian translation (hardback edition)

Beyond Done With The Crying: More Answers and Advice for Parents of Estranged Adult Children
ISBN—print: 978-0997352252; e-book: 978-0997352269
Silver Medal Winner: *IBPA's Benjamin Franklin Award*
Also available as a Tantor Media audiobook

Rumination Remedies: A Workbook to Free Your Mind From Worry, Regret, and Racing Thoughts
ISBN—print: 978-0997352276; e-book: 978-0997352283
A practical workbook with 40+ tools to quiet overthinking.
Translation forthcoming (Taiwan edition)

Done With The Crying Workbook for Parents of Estranged Adult Children
A companion to *Done With The Crying* (for e-book and audiobook readers, or those who want to revisit the exercises.)
ISBN—print: 978-0997352245

Nature's Healing Spirit: Real Life Stories to Nurture the Soul
ISBN—print: 978-0997352221; e-book: 978-0997352238
33 essays exploring the connection between nature
and well-being.